AF428245

Holly Celebrates Juneteenth

by Kimberly Kendall-Drucker

Holly Celebrates Juneteenth

Library of Congress Control Number: 2022906797

Hardback ISBN: 979-8-9859369-2-6

Paperback ISBN: 979-8-9859369-3-3

For the Ancestors –
including my grandmothers
Eunice and *Martelia* who persevered
even when their lives, to paraphrase
Langston Hughes, were *no crystal* stair.

Holidays are sprinkled through the year
Loaded with fun and folly.
I celebrate each one of them
Because my name is HOLLY!

Some Holly-Days are somber days -
And some are just plain fun.
Still, when your name is Holly
You LOVE each and everyone.

HOLLY
DAYS

JUNE
TEENTH
FREEDOM DAY
JUNETEENTH
CELEBRATION

June 19th marks a HOLLY-day
When **freedom is** celebrated.
Freedom delayed but not denied
To slaves who prayed and waited.

Juneteenth honors that outstanding day
When **all** slaves were finally free.
It is joyful! It is festive!
Here's how Juneteenth came to be.

Once a bright and beautiful people
Lived in a land they called their own.
They shared customs and religion
And they ruled themselves alone.

One day Evil landed on their shores
And brought with it disaster.
This Evil gave itself a name -
Demanding they call him Master.

They were stolen from their homeland.
Tossed on ships bound to be slaves.
Their journey was so frightening,
Some leaped over to watery graves.

Evil snatched them up from all they knew
Without a second thought -
Deciding these African people
Would be auctioned, sold, and bought.

Destined for America
Land of Free and Home of Brave -
But freedom's song did not apply
To the American Slave.

Slave Auction Today

Through blood and sweat and tears
Slaves planted indigo and cotton.
Yet the longing for their freedom
Could never ever be forgotten.

Then, Thursday, January 1st
Back in 1863,
Abraham Lincoln announced
That slaves, "**are now and henceforward shall be free.**"

If slaves toiled in the rebel states
With Confederate occupation –
Lincoln freed them through an Order
Called the Emancipation Proclamation.

Emancipation
Proclamation
I do order and declare that all persons
held as slaves within said designated
States and parts of States are and
henceforward shall be free [,] th
be done at appreciable compensation will be received
to the armed service of the United States
And upon this act sincerely believed
to be an act of justice war ranted by the
upon military necessity,
the considerate judgment of
mankind and the gracious favor of
Almighty God.
A. Lincoln.

And though it freed most of the slaves
It did not free them all
And some states – especially Texas –
Kept slaves to harvest cotton that fall.

No one gave the slaves the message.
There was no Snapchat or TikTok,
So they kept planting and chopping out in the fields
Working the cotton crops.

They didn't know in 1865
Freedom Day was coming soon
When Gordon Granger came to Texas
On the 19th day of June!

He brought a message from the Union
General Order Number Three,
And the words he read that day in Galveston
Meant all slaves would be free.

ALL SLAVES ARE FREE
GENERAL ORDER, NO 3
On June 19, 1865, Union Major-General Gordon Granger issued
this military order in Galveston, Texas, freeing slaves.
"THE PEOPLE OF TEXAS ARE INFORMED THAT, IN
ACCORDANCE WITH A PROCLAMATION FROM THE EXECUTIVE
OF THE UNITED STATES, ALL SLAVES ARE FREE."

The former slaves cried and rejoiced and danced.
They sang with jubilation!
We're free. We're free! We're Free! WE'RE FREE!
They shouted out with true elation!

They did not tread an easy path.
Sometimes they sang the blues,
But freedom allowed them all to sing
The songs they wished to choose.

On Juneteenth we lift our voices,
And we sing sweet freedom's song.
We honor our ancestors
Who lived in bondage oh so long.

JUNE
TEENTH
FREEDOM DAY

Now Juneteenth Jubilee Festivals
Happen in cities everywhere.
Mine has singing, laughing, and dancing
Food and fun for all to share.

There are speeches, dances, plays, and songs
From members of our community.
We sip strawberry soda and watch them all.
Juneteenth is a day about unity.

A Storyteller called a **Griot**
Narrates the history of this day
While African Dancers spin and twirl and stomp
To the beat of the Djembe.

I wrote a poem called "Liberty."
I'm performing it on stage.
It is all about the enslaved past
And how we turn the page.

To a tomorrow that's much brighter
Than all our yesterdays
And if our ancestors could see us now
How they would be amazed.

We are doctors and lawyers and teachers
And Supreme Court Justices too.
There is nothing that given our freedom
And an opportunity we cannot do.

We are writers and preachers and poets.
Even a President and a VP -
With the ancestors' spirit and blood in our veins
There is nothing that we cannot be.

If you cannot attend a festival
Don't you worry - not at all.
If you observe Juneteenth at home
You can still have a ball.

What's important is we **all** recognize -
Black Americans were not always free.
On Juneteenth we remember and celebrate
How that freedom came to be.

The End

Next in the Series:
Holly Celebrates Summer Vacation
Holly Celebrates Back to School

Although the **Emancipation Proclamation** and **General Order Number Three** (the Juneteenth Order) sought to end chattel slavery in the United States - the enslavement of Black people legally, permanently, and officially ended with the 13th Amendment.

The 13th Amendment to the Constitution
was ratified, December 6, 1865.

Thanks to the work of the **Grandmother of Juneteenth, Opal Lee** and myriad others - on June 17, 2021, President Joseph R. Biden signed a bill establishing **Juneteenth** as a National Holiday - celebrating and commemorating the end of slavery in the United States.

Kimberly Kendall-Drucker lives in Charlotte, North Carolina with her husband Larry and Persian kitty, Zuzu. She loves reading, and her books are her friends. Her favorite childhood books are *Where the Sidewalk Ends, Roll of Thunder Hear My Cry, A Wrinkle in Time,* and *Are You There, God? It's Me Margaret*. Kimberly reads a book a week – sometimes two. She is committed to writing accessible books children enjoy - because readers are leaders.

Kimberly loves *Phase 10*, macaroni and cheese, the Oxford Comma, and graphic tees. She is currently obsessed with *Wordle*. Jeopardy is her favorite TV show. While some people are outdoorsy, Kimberly is decidedly indoorsy. Still, she loves a day at the beach. For Kimberly, *family is everything*, and her nieces and nephews are her pride and joy.

Holly Celebrates Juneteenth is the fifth book in the Holly Celebrates Series and is Kimberly's sixth children's book.

To contact Kimberly or learn more about her, check out her website – **kimberlykendalldrucker.com**.